WEIRD AND AMAZING FACTS ABOUT FRENCH HISTORY AND CULTURE

GEORGE KENNEDY

FOREWORD AND ACKNOWLEDGEMENTS

This book is based entirely on historical facts with respect to the Republic of France. No part of it is to be considered fiction and all dating and figures are accurate.

TABLE OF CONTENT

George Kennedy

10. THE MIGOT LINE

11. KING LOUIS XIX LASTED JUST 20 MINUTES ON THE THRONE

12. THE NATIONAL BROTHERHOOD

13. THE FRENCH CAN WED A DEAD PERSON

14. THE FRENCH ARMY DID ONE THING FIRST

15. SEVERAL WORLD FAMOUS INVENTORS COME FROM FRANCE

16. WASTE OF FOOD IS ILLEGAL IN FRANCE

17. A MILLION FRENCH CITIZEN SPEAK ITALIAN AS NATIVE TONGUE

18. THE FRENCH HAVE BEEN BANNING OTHER LANGUAGES FOR 400 YEARS

19. RADIO STATIONS IN FRANCE ARE MORE THAN HALF FRENCH

20. THE FIRST MOVIE SHOOT WAS IN FRANCE

21. THE FRENCH LIVE LONGER THAN MOST PEOPLE

22. THE HIGHEST LAND AREA IN EUROPE IS LOCATED IN FRANCE

23. SAME-SEX MARRIAGE IS ALL LEGAL IN FRANCE

24. THE WORLD'S MOST FAMOUS MUSEUM IS IN FRANCE

George Kennedy

1 THE LAND OF FRANCE AND THE FRENCH

France is a large and very lovely country located in the western sector of Europe, with most of its shores bordering the Atlantic Ocean. It is an ancient land rich with fascinating history, traditions and culture. Hence, it is one of the most popular destinations for tourists from around the world. Additionally, due to its climate and geography, which are very health friendly, a lot of people living in the colder lands of northern Europe, the UK, and even Canada, tend to relocate to France for health reasons.

Are you about to travel to France for a very long vacation or perhaps, contemplating a permanent stay? In this book, we bring you some important facts about that wonderful nation that might help you on your way.

George Kennedy

2. FRANCE: AN ANCIENT AND MODERN SUPERPOWER

The official name of the nation of France is the French Republic (In French – *IRépublique Française*). France became a republic about 350 years ago after a massive uprising of the masses against their king and his nobles, an event that came to be known historically as the **French Revolution**.

The French Revolution took place in the year 1792 and saw the near-complete eradication of the French royal and ruling-class.

In the past, for several centuries, France was a superpower that battled Britain and Spain for world dominance. It had vast armies and fleets of the latest merchant and naval vessels that roamed the seas. There was a time, just a few centuries ago, when half of North America (present-day Canada), half of Africa (North Africa in particular) and large parts of Asia belonged to France. These lands were regarded as colonies (or territories of France) and were ruled over by what was known as the French colonial government (most of these regions still speak French as an official language today). In those days, the sun never went down on the empire that was France and the only other empires that could rival it was the British and the Spanish empires.

Today, that empire is gone, but not all of it.

Modern France currently retains possession of 15 territories overseas, including Guadeloupe, Martinique,

French Guiana, Mayotte, and Réunion. On the mainland itself, Metropolitan France (Corsica included) is divided into 13 separate regions, which are, in turn, sub-divided into 96 departments.

France's colonial past is the main reason why the country has a population of more than five million citizens of African and Arab descent.

Interestingly, France still retains a place as a world power in the modern world. It's a nuclear and financial power that manufactures its own brand of high-tech jets and ships for commercial and military use.

France ranks as both a military and economic superpower alongside the United States, Britain, Russia and China.

Economy

The French economy ranks as the second-largest in the Eurozone, right after that of Germany, suppressing even Britain and Spain. France is one of the world's largest exporters of luxury goods, with the leading four companies Chanel, Cartier, Hermes and Louis Vuitton raking in billions of dollars on a yearly basis. The main exports from France include food, aircraft, industrial machinery, chemicals, iron and steel, motor vehicles, electronics, and pharmaceuticals.

George Kennedy

Population

At present, France has a population of about 66 million and three-quarters of those people live in urban areas, with Paris, the capital city of the nation, having about 3 million inhabitants alone.

Metropolitan Paris, which comprises of all the surrounding suburbs of Paras, is home to about 12 million people, reports the French national statistical office (the United Nations has a slightly lower figure). This makes France the second most populated country in Europe; Germany occupies the number one spot.

The population of France makes up about 13 percent of the total population of the European Union and around 0.85% of the world's total population.

Normally, birth rates in the Eurozone are quite low, with the average woman having just 1.6 children in her lifetime. The highest birth-rates of the zone are to be found in Ireland (16.876 births per thousand people per year) and France. (13.013 births per thousand people per year).

According to OECD reports, France was only recently displaced by Ireland in the ranking of nations with the highest birth rates.

Living Standards

The living standard in France is among one of the best in the world. In fact, the life-work balance ratio in the country ranks 12th among all OECD nations and 4th in Europe behind the Netherlands, Sweden and Denmark.

French workers tend to retire a lot younger than those in the other OECD nations. A recent report from the OECD puts the average French retirement age at 59 years, compared to the average OECD figure of 64.2 years. In France, people may lay claim to state-retirement benefits at just 62 years of age, and this is one of the lowest ages of retirement in the world.

The Stats

Outlined below are some statistics and values that shed some more light on the nation we are going to be talking about in this book…. France. All are based on the current year 2019.

- The total land area of France is 547,557 km2 (or 211,413 sq. miles)
- The total population of France, as of Friday, February 1, 2019, stands at 65,378,748. This value is based on the most recent United Nations estimates.
- The population of France is equivalent to about 0.85% of the world's total population.

George Kennedy

- The nation of France is ranked number 22 in the list of nations (and dependencies) by population.
- The overall population density on the French mainland is 120 per Km2 (or 310 people per mi2).
- About 81.4 % of the population live in urban areas (as of 2019 that number stands at 53,298,174 people.)
- The median age in France is 41.4 years.

The Fascinating Facts Begin

Now that we are better informed on basic facts about France lets dig a little deeper into the nation's fascinating history and culture.

3. THE FRENCH REVOLUTION CHANGED ALL

It took place in 1792, a war of sorts. It was a fearsome uprising of the French common people against their king, against centuries of royal rule.

Once, there are many magnificent castles in France. They were home to the French kings and wealthy nobles (Dukes, Earls, Lords) who ruled France until the people rose up against them in revolt, a struggle that became known as the French Revolution.

The revolution completely wiped out the royalty and nobility of France. Most of them were killed by the people and those who survived did so by escaping into exile in other lands.

All the nobles and royalties of France, from the king down, lost their wealth, lands and titles in the French revolution. Everything became the property of the people, the citizens of the newly born Republic of France, including the castles which are, today, massive tourist attractions.

The image below shows one of the most impressive castles of France. It is bordered to the north and east by lovely canals.

George Kennedy

Image 1: A French Castle still in very good shape.

The Revolution began with the French people storming the famous fortress of Bastille on the 14th day of July 1789, an event which is celebrated much like an independence every year all over the country and it's known as Bastille Day.

The Bastille (in French: *bastij*) was a large fortress in Paris, that was formally and famously as the *Bastille Saint-Antoine*. It featured prominently in the domestic conflicts of France and the kings of France used it

mainly as a state prison for important citizens.

The Bastille was originally built by the French kings to defend their capital city of Paris from the terrible invasions of the English in what became known as the *Hundred Years' War*. The foundations were first laid in 1357, but the work never quite ended for one more century as the structure was transformed into a strong fortress with eight massive towers that guarded the strategic gateway of the Porte Saint-Antoine located on the eastern edge of the city of Paris.

The design of the fortress proved so successful that it was widely copied throughout Europe.

On 14 July 1789, following an uprising against the economic depression and civil unrest of the time, the fortress was attacked by crowds of common people in what turned out to become the French Revolution. It was later demolished and the Place de la Bastille, built in its place.

Today, there's nothing left of the Bastille fortress except some parts of its massive stone foundation that were moved to the side of Boulevard Henri IV.

George Kennedy

4. THE NAPOLEONIC ERA

The Napoleonic Era was one of the greatest Eras ever witnessed in French history as it was a time when France almost conquered the entire world much like Germany nearly did under Hitler and the Nazis in World War 2 (1939 -1945).

The French dominated Europe and the rest of the world under their famous hero, General Napoleon Bonaparte (1769 - 1821).

Rising through the ranks of the French Army toward the end period of the French revolution, Napoleon went from one national victory to the other until he finally got promoted to full General, ceased absolute power and became a military dictator. Next, hc attempted to conquer the entire world, beginning with Europe.

It was not Russia, not mighty Spain, but the English, protectively surrounded by the seas and backed by their vast naval fleet, that presented Napoleon with the toughest challenge and he finally met defeat at the **battle of Waterloo**.

Ever heard a phrase such as… "He will soon meet his Waterloo, or she will soon meet her Waterloo"? Now you know where they come from.

Though an ancient figure, this General, Napoleon, is responsible for a lot of changes in France such as in its legal system, most of which held firm even today. Perhaps one of the most famous is the aspect that deals with crimes. In France, unlike other western lands, the accused is presumed guilty until proven innocent. So you might want to be very careful to stay within the law when next you pay a visit to France because once accused or suspected of any crime, you'll be arrested and jailed even before that crime is investigated in any way.

George Kennedy

5. FRANCE IS THE NUMBER ONE DESTINATION FOR TOURISTS AROUND THE WORLD

From North and South America, they come. From Africa, from Australia, from Asia and all over Europe, they come in their millions, the tourists of the world and their number one destination is France!

France is a large and very lovely country that is immensely rich in history, traditions and culture that quite old and so it has a lot to offer tourists, from old castles and towering monuments to some of the most amazingly beautiful natural sceneries in the world (we will be discussing most of these features in this book). However, the number one thing France has to offer that everyone wants the most but can get nowhere else is in the form of a very lovely and very old city… **Paris**, the capital of France!

Image 2: The city of Paris

Image 3: The French Alps. Highest Mountains in Europe

George Kennedy

Image 4: An all-white house French city perched high on a mountain overlooking the sea

Image 5: The gateway to a region of very lovely natural scenery in France.

Image 6: City in Southern France

Paris has a lot of fascinating things to offer the millions of tourists that flock to it each year, from historical sites to an amazing array of five-star hotels and restaurants. More importantly, Paris is both the fashion and love capital of the world. Everyone wants to go shopping in Paris, particularly women, and so many couples around the world want to visit there either to tie up the knot, honeymoon or have a memorable anniversary of their union. The result? Millions and millions of people pay a visit to Paris yearly.

Most tourist destinations around the world have peak and off seasons, but Paris and indeed, the rest of France, do not. Whatever time of the year it is the visitors can be seen all over the city and the streets and hotels are jam-packed with them.

According to the World Tourism Organization, for 2013-16, about 85 million people visit France each year, making it the most-visited country in the world. However, in 2018, France crept passed that record with a total of over

George Kennedy

89 million tourists visiting the country. Interestingly, the city of Paris drew more than half of that figure.

The total number of tourists that visited Greater Paris alone in 2018 exceeded 40 million, reports the Paris tourist office. The city currently rakes in an estimated 19 billion dollars each year from tourist spending alone.

Lyon, Lille, Nice, Bordeaux, Strasbourg, Toulouse, Saint-Malo, Annecy, Riquewihr, Colmar, Chamonix, Aix-en-Provence, Marseille, Montpellier, Nantes, and Montpellier. Excluding Paris, these cities are the top tourist destinations in France. Nowhere else in the world will you find a collection of breathtaking scenery and beauty like you will find in these French cities.

Simply put, when it comes to tourism, France leads and the rest of the world follow.

6. BUILDERS OF MASSIVE MONUMENTS

A monument is a large structure such as a stone statue, carving: or anything designed and built (erected) as a lasting public tribute to a memorable event, a person, or a group of people.

The most famous monuments in the world today were built ages ago and one of the countries that had the best craftsmen for this job was France.

Image 7: The Eiffel Tower in central Paris France.

Construction and Structure

- Construction began – 28 January 1887

George Kennedy

- Project Completed – 15 March 1889
- Opened to Public – 31 March 1889 (129 years ago)
- Height of Tip from ground – 324 m (1,063 ft)
- Official Height of Structure – 324 meters (1,063 ft)
- Number of Floor Levels – 3
- Height of Top Floor Level from Ground – 276 m (906 ft)
- Number of Lifts/elevators – 8
- Owner of Structure – City of Paris, France

The Eiffel Tower (pronounced: *EYE-fəl*) is a huge wrought-iron lattice tower situated on the lovely gardened grounds known as the Champ de Mars in central Paris, France. It is so named after the talented French engineer Gustave Eiffel, whose construction company designed and built it entirely from the ground up.

The tower was constructed as the entrance to the 1889 World's Fair, which took place in France at the time, and initially came under heavy criticism from some of France's leading intellectuals and artists for its alleged substandard design, but in no time, it became loved by the French people. Today, the structure stands as a global cultural icon of the nation of France and one of the most famous structures in the world.

The Eiffel Tower is currently the most-visited paid monument on earth. It has an estimated 8 million people ascending it each year. Unfortunately, the top floor of the tower is only accessible to citizens of the European Union so if you are coming in from any other continent, just be aware of the limitations.

A Record Breaker

Standing at 324 meters (1,063 ft), the Eiffel tower is about as tall as an 81-storey building and is definitely the tallest structure in the city of Paris. It has a wide square base measuring 125 meters (410 ft) on each side.

This tower is so high that it can be seen from all over Paris. Unsurprisingly, it can be seen clearly towering above Paris in almost any photo taken of the city. See image 2 above.

The Eiffel tower ranks as one of the tallest man-made structure in the entire world, surpassing the Washington Monument and the Chrysler Building in New York City.

Lady Liberty

There are other massive monuments in France, all constructed by skilled French craftsmen, but perhaps the most interesting of all these French constructions is one that stands thousands of miles outside France… the **Statue of Liberty**.

George Kennedy

Yeah, you heard right. The French actually built the Statue of Liberty as a gift to the United States in the days when it first got independence from Britain. The statue was built wholly in France during the 1870s and shipped to the United States in pieces. There it was assembled and erected in the place it stands today… Liberty Island.

7. THE CITY OF LIGHTS

The city of Paris is sometimes called **The City of Light** (in French: ***La Ville Lumière***) but not many know why. The reason for this unusual name is that the city played a leading role during the era, or rather, the Age of Enlightenment.

However, some local historians also hold that the nickname is there because Paris was one of the first major cities in Europe to use gas street lighting on a grand scale on its monuments and boulevards

What is a Boulevard?
A Boulevard is simply the French native name for their streets and avenues. But it's just not every street or avenue, though. The name is used especially for wide streets lined with trees or gardens. So when next you visit France and hear a name that sounds much like 'Louis Boulevard" just know that you are looking for a spectacular looking broad road by the name of Louis that's lined with trees or gardens.

George Kennedy

8. FRANCE: THE LARGEST COUNTRY IN THE EUROPEAN UNION

It may not be as quite as populated as Germany or as large as the United States, South Africa or India, but France, with an area of 551,000 sq. km is the largest nation in the European Union. It is something of a hexagonally shaped nation that occupies almost a fifth of the EU's total land area – France has a six-sided shape.

9. FRANCE IS HEAVILY FORESTED

One of the most attractive features of France is its forests. About a quarter of the total land mass of the country is covered by thick forest; only Finland and Sweden have more.

Image 8: A lovely town in South France.

During the latter part of the Second World War, when the Allied forces got the upper hand over Germany, the Germans build some of the most extensive underground bunkers in the forests of France and even till today, some of them are still being discovered.

George Kennedy

10. THE MIGOT LINE

You don't always hear about it now, but it's right there in France and a major part of the nation's history.

In the years leading up to the Second World War, with Germany's military powers growing by the day, France built a line of mighty forts manned by its soldiers to protect itself from air and land assaults from the deeper lands of Europe where Germany lay.

In its day, the Migot line was regarded as impregnable until the British began to overfly it at will with their new warplanes and then the American Air Force joined them. In the end, the Germans came calling as well in the person of General Romenel and his lightning-fast armored Panzer divisions.

Coming from an odd region of Europe after making all kinds of detours through other European countries that saw them cross impossible rivers and swamps, the Germans hit the Migot line from behind where its massive guns were not guarding and overran it in one single day. And that was how France, one of Europe's superpowers at the time, fell to the Germans without a fight. Technically, the French military machinery was still asleep when the Germans hit and defeated them.

The fall of the Migot line put an end to the use of fortresses for defense in modern warfare.

11. KING LOUIS XIX LASTED JUST 20 MINUTES ON THE THRONE

The French King Louis XIX ruled France for just 20 minutes before he died. His was the shortest reign ever–he ascended to the French royal throne in July 1830 right after his father Charles X abdicated. The new king abdicated himself 20 minutes afterward in favor of his young nephew, the Duke of Bordeaux.

Interestingly, King Louis XIX shares this unusual record with the Crown Prince Luís Filipe, who briefly become king of all Portugal after the assassination of his father but died from a battle wound 20 minutes later.

George Kennedy

12. THE NATIONAL BROTHERHOOD

The motto of France, *Liberté, égalitié, fraternité* means 'liberty, equality and fraternity' (or simply brotherhood). It first showed up around the time of the French Revolution, which took place between 1789–1799, and was then written into the constitutions of 1946 and 1958.

In France today, you'll see it on postage stamps, coins, and even government logos. It often appears alongside '*Marianne*' who represents the 'triumph of the Republic'. The present French legal system is still hugely based on the principles laid down during Napoleon Bonaparte's Code Civil right after the revolution, in the 1800s.

13. THE FRENCH CAN WED A DEAD PERSON

In France, according to standing French laws, you can marry a dead person.

In exceptional cases, one can legally marry a dead body. As long as that person can prove that the deceased originally had the intention of marrying him or her while alive, that person can seek and receive permission from the president of France to get married.

The most recent case in which a presidential approval was granted, took place in 2017 when the lover of a gay policeman who was gunned down by a jihadist on Paris's Champs-Elysees was granted special permission to marry his partner posthumously.

George Kennedy

14. THE FRENCH ARMY DID ONE THING FIRST

The French Army was the very first army in the world to make use of camouflage and they did so during World War 1 back in 1915. The word camouflage originates from the French verb *'to make up for the stage'*.

So how was this done back then? It was quite simple. Vehicles and guns meant for war were carefully painted over by artists known as *camofleurs*.

15. SEVERAL WORLD FAMOUS INVENTORS COME FROM FRANCE

With a history and society so rich, it is not surprising that France has produced several world-renowned inventions. For example, in 1809 confectioner Nicolas Appert, known as the 'father of canning', came up with the idea of using sealed glass jars placed in hot boiling water as a means to preserve food. Of course, this later led to the use of tin cans in place of the glass jars, but guess who thought of that too? Another Frenchman named Pierre Durand.

The writing and reading system for the blind, called Braille, was developed by a French citizen by the name of Louis Braille who was blinded as a little child. A French physician René Laennec is credited for inventing the stethoscope at a top hospital in Paris back in 1816. He first discovered the unusual technique to listen directly to heartbeats by rolling up a paper into a tube.

Another Frenchman, Alexandre-Ferdinand Godefroy's patented contraption was the first and only hair dryer on earth as of 1888. The Montgolfier brothers Etienne and Joseph became the pioneers of hot air flight after the world was held spellbound in 1783 by their first public showing of an untethered hot air balloon. A little known fact is that one of the world's most popular games, Etch-a-Sketch was actually invented in France during the 1950s after André Cassagnes, a smart French electrical technician, peeled away a translucent transfer from the plate of a light

George Kennedy

switch and found that his pencil marks were still there on its underside, a direct result of the metallic powder which was electrostatically charged.

16. WASTE OF FOOD IS ILLEGAL IN FRANCE

The French Government was the first in the world to ban supermarkets in the country from destroying or throwing away unsold food. The law, which went into full effect in February 2016, requires shops to donate wastage to charities or food banks.

Image 9: An open French Food market doing a giveaway.

Perhaps this law is the reason the French are so generous with food, even to strangers. Whoever you go to in France, never will you see food wastage but always giveaways.

George Kennedy

17. A MILLION FRENCH CITIZEN SPEAK ITALIAN AS NATIVE TONGUE

More than one million French citizens who live near the French border with Italy speak Italian as a native tongue. Although French is France's official language and the native tongue (first language) of more than 88 percent of the country's population, there are numerous indigenous regional languages and dialects, such as Basque, Alsacian, Breton, Occitan, Flemish and Catalan.

Interestingly, French is actually Europe's second most spoken mother tongue. German is first and English is third. Experts predict that French will become the number one language in Europe by the year 2025 due to that country's phenomenal high birth rate.

George Kennedy

18. THE FRENCH HAVE BEEN BANNING OTHER LANGUAGES FOR 400 YEARS

The sole aim of a major governmental group or agency in France known as the *Académie Française* is to preserve the French language and this group of officials has been in existence since 1634.

The agency carries out its duties by attempting to ban everything associated with foreign words such as website and blogs, emails, hashtags, parking areas, and weekend trips. This group was founded by a small clique of French intellectuals and in 1635, King Louis XIII officially recognized them, but in all that time, till today, they have not been successful in their endeavors.

19. RADIO STATIONS IN FRANCE ARE MORE THAN HALF FRENCH

By French law, no less than 40 percent of all music aired on all private radio stations within the country must be French in origin. This has been so since 1996, and the law is enforced by the *Conseil Supérieur de L'Audiovisuel* (CSA), the country's top media regulatory body.

The CSA goes a step further to keep things a bit old fashioned and traditional through the requirement that at least half of the French music quota aired be less than six months old.

There you go! When next you turn on your radio while in France, don't be surprised at the kind of music you hear.

George Kennedy

20. THE FIRST MOVIE SHOOT WAS IN FRANCE

The world's first public screening of a movie took place in France on 28th December 1895 and was done by the French brothers Louis and Auguste Lumière.

The brothers made use of their invention, which they called *cinématographe* (translated 'cinema'), to feature 10 films, each lasting about 50 seconds, at the Salon Indien du Grand Café in Paris.

As history is a witness, the Lumière brothers went on to make a lot of other films, but wrongly predicted that the 'cinema was an invention with no future'

21. THE FRENCH LIVE LONGER THAN MOST PEOPLE

A French woman who lived in France holds the record as the world's oldest human being ever. According to the Guinness Book of World Records, she lived up to the incredible age of 122 years and 164 days.

Jeanne Louise Calment, born 21 February 1875, passed away on 4 August 1997. She lived through the famous opening of the Eiffel Tower in 1889, the first and second World Wars and the development of the television, the modern motor vetches, and aircraft!

Interestingly, her case is not that strange because French citizens, due to the high health standards and the natural beauty and purity of their country, generally live a lot longer than most people in other lands:

Image 12: A typical house in France.

George Kennedy

If you've ever visited any French town or city before you will understand what we are trying to convey here. Simply put, the people of France coexist with nature a lot more than the people of other nations; even Japan and the United States were planting trees and gardens is a habit does not come close to France. In France, the plants, gardens and trees are everywhere, on the streets, bridges, squares, parks, public buildings and even in private homes. There is almost no city without lovely canals of fresh water flowing through it for boats to travel by or narrow roads that encourage people to do more walking rather than driving. A typical swimming pool in France is surrounded by thick bushes of lovely plants and vegetable gardens are what you have around homes.

All these plants and trees work constantly to purify the air people breath and produce fresh vegetables and other foods for them to eat. The walking and boating ensure that people stay healthy and also breathe clean air. This method of life is the exact opposite of what is in other developed lands where everyone owns a car and, with no trees in the cities, the air is suffocating with pollution. Little wonder the people of France are so healthy and the air referred to as sweet in that country.

France is currently rated fifth in the OECD countries for life expectancy after birth – the total figure for that nation stands at 79 years for men and 85 years for women.

22. THE HIGHEST LAND AREA IN EUROPE IS LOCATED IN FRANCE

The highest mountain in Europe is Mount Blanc and it is located in the French Alps. At 4,810 meters high, it takes one an arduous 11 to 13 hours to climb up to the summit of Mount Blanc. Alternatively, one can take a pleasant 20-minute vertical trip up on Europe's highest cable car located on the nearby Aiguille du Midi and get a thrilling view of Mont Blanc.

23. SAME-SEX MARRIAGE IS ALL LEGAL IN FRANCE

At a time when even the world's top courts are ruling that same-sex marriage is directed at the extinction of the human race and so cannot be legalized, France has legalized same-sex marriage. This became official when French President Françoise Holland signed the controversial bill into law on 18th May 2013. France, from then on, became the ninth country within Europe and the 14th in the world to recognize and legalize same-sex marriage.

At that time, the country's polls showed that about 50% of French citizens supported gay marriage, but, surprisingly, so many showed their displeasure at the development. Thousands of protesters took to the streets to defend wholesome family values.

George Kennedy

24. THE WORLD'S MOST FAMOUS MUSEUM IS IN FRANCE

Located in the heart of Paris is the Louvre Museum and according to standing records, it is the most visited museum in the world. Back in 2014 alone, it had a stunning 9.3 million visitors, this figure is roughly equivalent to the current population of Sweden.

25. THE FIRST FACE AND HEART TRANSPLANT OCCURRED IN FRANCE

The very first artificial face transplant and heart transplant the world had ever seen both took place in France. Surgeons in France were the first to contemplate, and then perform, a face transplant, which took place in 2005.

The case of the heart transplant was more complex and it took place in December 2013 at the Georges Pompidou Hospital in Paris. The newly invented bioprosthetic device, which imitated the activities of a real heart, was powered by external lithium-ion batteries and is about three times heavier than a real heart.

George Kennedy

26. EUROPE'S BUSIEST RAILWAY STATION IS IN FRANCE

In Paris is the bustling *Paris Gare du Nord* and according to records, it is, by far, the busiest railway station in all of Europe, with no less than 190 million passengers going through each and every year.

The station, which was set up a year after the Second World War (1946), is one of the world's oldest railway stations.

27. THE FRENCH RAIL NETWORK IS A COMPLICATED AFFAIR

With a total of 29,000km, the French rail network ranks as the second biggest in Europe (Germany is first) and the ninth largest in the entire world. With the introduction of the TGV high-speed rail in 1981, France became one of the first countries in the World to utilize high-speed rail technology.

The Tours-Bordeaux high-speed project, which is due for completion in 2018-20, will inject a further 302km to the already existing 1,550km of the high-speed rail network.

One glaring point of failure here was the action of the SNCF, France's national train operators, in ordering 2,000 expensive trains, all at a staggering cost of 15 billion Euros, only to find out in 2014 that they were too wide for most of the regional platforms.

George Kennedy

28. FRENCH WINE ARE HIDEOUSLY EXPENSIVE

In the entire world, the only wines that climb to astronomical prices for little or no reasons are French wines.

In the latter part of 2014, Sotheby's auctioned off a 114-bottle lot of DCR Romanee-Conti wines over in Hong Kong for a staggering EUR 1.45m. The sale went down as a world record for a single wine lot, but the Asia-based buyer chose to remain anonymous.

Technically, the wine works out to approximately nine thousand euros per bottle or about one thousand, six hundred and nineteen euros per glass!

29. THE METRIC SYSTEM ORIGINATED IN FRANCE

The metric system, the decimalized method of weighing and counting internationally, was invented by the French in 1793.

The original prototype that was used was very unique; it was known as the kilo or Le Grand K, a cylinder made in the late 1880s out of platinum and iridium and it was about the size of a plum. This object was the only object ever known to scientists to have a precise mass of just one kilogram. Everything that's ever measured in kilograms is actually defined by the French's unique Le Grand K.

The Le Grand K is kept locked away in three airtight (vacuum-sealed) bell jars within a large vault in the BIPM, France's International Bureau of Weights and Measures, which, unsurprisingly, is located in Sevres, a lovely sector of Paris, France.

Later, duplicate cylinders were sent out around the world and from time to time they're compared to the original cylinder. Unfortunately, Le Grand K mysteriously appears to be losing weight: The last time its caretakers weighed it, in 1988, it was discovered to be short of 0.05 milligrams (this is a weight less than a grain of sugar). Nonetheless, this makes it slightly lighter than the duplicates around the world.

Did the copies gain weight or did Le Grand K just lose it instead? No one really knows.

George Kennedy

30. THE FRENCH ACT OF PREPARING AND EATING FOOD IS ONE OF THE BEST IN THE WORLD

In 2010, French gastronomy got bestowed with UNESCO World Heritage Status–it was added to the unique list of 'imperceptible cultural heritage of humanity'.

Image 11: The food! It's always the first thing that gets you when you visit France.

According to experts, the importance of French gastronomy as 'a social custom', is aimed at celebrating the most significant moments in the lives of groups of people and individuals'. It's also important for its function in 'emphasizing union' such as bringing family and friends closer together and also strengthening social ties.

George Kennedy

31. THE FRENCH LOVE CYCLING

The greatest cycle race in the world, the Tour de France, has been in existence for more than 100 years. The first event was held on the first day of July 1903. Since then, each July, cyclists come together to race more than 3,200km (2,000 miles), a journey that takes them around France in a series of stages spanning over 23 days, and the fastest cyclist at each stage gets to wear the famous yellow jersey.

George Kennedy

32. FRENCH WRITERS ARE AMONG THE BEST IN THE WORLD

Some of the world's most influential thinkers and writers come from France. They include Pascal and Descartes in the 17th century, Voltaire in the 18th, Flaubert and Baudelaire in the 19th and Camus and Sartre in the 20th. Till date, France has won the most Noble Prizes for Literature: no less than 15 Frenchmen have won it. No other nation in the world can boast of more.

33. THE LONGEST NOVEL IN WORLD IS OF FRENCH ORIGIN

The French writer and poet, Marcel Proust holds the world record of having the longest novel to his name. The novel, *la recherche du temps perdu* is a 13-volume masterpiece, which was translated as the book *Remembrance of things past*, is well over 3,000 pages long and has a cast of hundreds and thousands of interwoven plot strands.

The first volume of this novel was published in the year1913.

George Kennedy

34. FRENCH CHEESE IS WORLD CLASS

The French produce about a billion tons of cheese each year and these come in 1,200 different varieties! Cheese making is an ancient art in France that began with: goats cheese and dates back to about 500AD.

The French blue-veined Roquefort cheese was mentioned in the records of an ancient monastery in Conques as early as 1070, and hand farmed cheeses such as Emmental began to show up in the early 1200s.

A French axiom goes… 'there's literally a different cheese for each day in the year'. The original French words go like this '*un fromage par jour par de l'année'*. I don't write French that well mind you, so don't hold me responsible for any errors in translation, but hey, the class and pride of these people are truly something to behold!

35. APRIL FOOL'S DAY ORIGINATED IN FRANCE

The celebration of April fool's day in France is so big that one can get a 'certain kind' of fish glued onto your back on such a day.

If you happen to be in France on the first of April, don't be surprised if kids try to stick paper fish to your back with some glue and then declare you a *'Poisson d'Avril'* (April Fish).

This tradition dates way back to the 16th century, when French King Charles XIV changed the calendar and those citizens who continued to celebrate the end of the Year at the end of the month of March were ridiculed as fools.

George Kennedy

36. THE FIRST VOICE RECORDING WAS IN FRANCE

On 9 April 1860, a French inventor named Edouard-Leon Scott de Martinville recorded the first human voice on paper– it was a 10-second fragment of the song Au Clair de la Lune and today stands as the oldest recording in the world.

So how did he do it?

Edouard used a 'phonautograph', an instrument which allowed sounds to be recorded visually on paper. That paper recording, after going missing for so long, was finally discovered in Paris in 2008, and with the aid of modern science, the clip was processed and played for the first time ever.

37. SNAILS ARE A CHERISHED DELICACY IN FRANCE

While wild snails are something of a problem in countries like Australia, the French love it. They consume about 30,000 tons of snails each year to prove that. However, less than 1,000 tons of this classic French delicacy (which is eaten with parsley, garlic, and butter) come from France. As of 2016, the number of registered snail farms in France was less than 100. So where do the rest of the snails come from? They are imported from other lands including Europe and Africa.

Eastern Europe accounts for most of France's snail imports. Strangely enough, the snails are not grown on farms, but plucked from the forests, fields and roadsides of the rural regions of those lands.

Africa, which accounts for the rest of France's snail imports, has a taste for the delicacy as well. Most African tribes value snails very highly and the land is blessed with a species of snail that is the largest on earth; the Giant African Snail. There are a number of snail farms in West Africa that ship their products to France regularly but, as in Eastern Europe, much of the snails are gotten from the wild; the forest, bushy fields and roadsides.

Perhaps it's worth mentioning here that decades ago, someone tried to start snail farming Giant African snails in a part of the forested lands of Australia. The result? Pure disaster!

No one knows exactly who brought the Giant African snail to Australia, but the snails got out of hand quickly and escaped into the wild. Unchecked by their natural predators, the snails began to multiply at an alarming rate, destroying gardens and food crops on farms (snails feed on vegetation). When the rains fell, the snails got washed out from the forests onto isolated roads in abundance, making the terrain extremely slippery with their slime as they got crushed under the tires of speeding vehicles. This led to so many accidents because vehicles lost traction on such roads, particularly at night. Eventually, the government and people had to treat the snail issue as that of a pest to get it under some control.

George Kennedy

38. DOMESTICATED ANIMALS MUST HAVE THEIR OWN TRAIN TICKETS

By French law, certain animals much have their own train tickets to board a train. Take snails, for example, it is against the law for a person to carry live snails on a high-speed train without purchasing their own tickets. Any domesticated animal under the weight of 5 kilograms, by French law, must be a paying passenger. In 2008, a Frenchman was charged to court and fined for carrying snails on a TGV without tickets. That the fine was later waived didn't change the law.

39. THE FASHION POLICE

Most people have not heard the term 'fashion police' before, but in France, you will.

France, the world's leading center of fashion, is home to a lot of fashion-oriented companies that manufacture and sell everything from clothes, shoes and bags, to sportswear, sunglasses and jewelry. As such, French law takes the undermining presence of fake products in this sector very seriously.

In France, if you are ever caught in possession of any fake fashion product, even if it's just the one handbag you are carrying or the one shirt you are wearing, you will definitely end up in jail.

40. FINAL WORD

Now that you know a lot about French History and Culture, still want to go to France? Good idea. Try to make a booking with one of their top travel agencies to get the best out of your visit.

The End

Author's Note

The world is a huge place and like an interesting movie, it has been playing out in a series of fascinating tales for thousands of years. Many people call it history, but I just call it 'fascinating real-life tales' and write books in that light exactly.

My current books are…

1. **The Amazons: Lives and Legends of Warrior Queens and Warrior Women of Ancient Times.**
2. **Weird and Amazing Facts About French History and Culture**

Coming soon…
1. The Most Wicked and Evil Women in History

All my works will be published and promoted by Kingbooks. It will also be featured on
www.kingexesblog.com
Stay with me.

Author
George Kennedy

George Kennedy

FIND OTHER BOOKS BY THE AUTHOR

All book by the Author can be found on the publisher's websites listed below.

George Kennedy

ABOUT THE PUBLISHER

Kingbooks is a brand under which a group of talented authors and intellectuals self-publish books in the different genres. We maintain a presence on the website of the founding author of the brand.

Visit Our Website Home page: Kingezesblog.com
Visit Our Web Page:
https://kingezesblog.com/kingbooks

Kingbooks: Entertainment and knowledge are our trade and we publish only the best books.

NOTES

George Kennedy

NOTES